A Journey of Emotions

Christina George

Presentation by *BookLeaf Publishing*

Web: www.bookleafpub.com

E-mail: info@bookleafpub.com

ISBN: 9789357212564

First edition 2023

PREFACE

These poems came to me in a variety of ways. They are based on things I went through and things I tired to help my family and friends through.

Seclusion

Sitting in a room full of laughter.
Yet somehow secluded in silence.
Surrounded by friends.
Still strangely all alone.
Running towards the light, but always far
behind.
No matter what you try, there is no way to join
Those happy faces and cheerful voices, that
surround you everyday.
To know your fate is sealed, but unaware of the
crime.
The sentence seclusion....from this day on.
There is no way to fight it, and no use in
questioning it.
Nothing you do will lift it.
Ask anything you want, they won't explain it.
All you can do is live it.
From this day on.

As I Sit

As I sit and stare, hoping he was here.
Always dreaming about him.
Still always in despair.
Walking in a different direction.
Never looking his way.
Our eyes never lock, they never meet.
We never speak, nor does he know my name.
Teardrops fall when I see him with another girl.
Time passes slowly when he's not near.
A day feels like a week, a week is like a year.
The way he walks, the way he talks, all bring
smiles upon my face.
My hearts been in two since I saw his eyes so
blue.
When he smiles it puts me in a trance.
Standing frozen, paralyzed in joy.
Hoping this feeling will never die.
Knowing some day it will end.

Broken Glass

Too much happened, can't start anew.
Too much pain to part as friends.
Broken promises are easier forgotten.
Yet a broken heart tames time to mend.
Smiles dampened and laughter ceased.
Trust is shattered piece by piece.
A glass heart broken by the lies.
Slowly the spirit withers and dies.

Lullaby of Night

Darkness wraps around me, a soft and warm
blanket.
It's familiar embrace comforts me.
The moon appears and the stars start to shine.
Soft sounds of crickets join the oil's haunting
call.
It lulls me to sleep as the midnight hour begins
to fall.
My lullaby of night continues until the sun does
rise.

Cruel Emotions

I feel the anger building up.
I feel my heart tearing at the seams.
Things aren't always how they appear.
Look at me, what so you think you see?
Sadness is creeping up at me.
Anger is fighting to be free.
My emotions are running wild.
I feel just like a little child.
My heart can't take much more.
My spirit needs to soar.
Higher than ever before.

Gone Not Forgotten

Gone but not forgotten.
Your voice echoes when I hear your favorite
song.
The wind carries the smell of your perfume on
the breeze.
Far from forgotten.
Bubbles float around my mind.
Each one a treasured memory.
They can never be forgotten.
Gone for now is not goodbye forever.
Just until we meet again.

After Today

After today who is going to help me whenever
I'm down?
After today I'm on my own.
Will I have to face the world alone?
After today will someone be by my side.
If I have a problem, will any one try to help?
After today what will they all say?
After today....

Forget

Forget the way he held you close
Whenever the wind blew cold.
Forget the way he kissed your cheek.
Each and every time you'd cry.
Forget the way he made you feel.
When you danced the night away.
Forget the way you're day would brighten.
With his whispered, "I love you."
Most of all forget the way you're heart broke.
When he just walked away.

Trapped

I'm trapped inside.
I can't let my feelings out.
Anger and sadness keep building up.
Scared to let my feelings out.
I feel the love and joy inside.
But I won't let anyone know.
What I feel and hide inside.

Within

A troubled soul lies deep within.
A shattered heart that tries not to break.
While tear filled eyes try not to cry.

Wary

There's a sadness in your eyes.
One that makes you wary of making ties.
Built on a foundation of lies.
I know the feelings.that you're hiding.
The pain that comes from always denying.
Learning to trust again is trying.
Take it one step at a time.
First you learn, then you confide.
Have your courage intensified.

Words

Three little words with so much power.
Three simple words, and your world collapses.
Your knees give out as the the ground crumbles.
Every breath is stolen from your lungs.
You want to cry, but you're eyes are dry.
All you can do is say why? Why? Why?

Whole

Broken bones and a trampled spirit.
An empty shell of my former self.
Piece by piece I fixed what was broken.
Years drifted by and I survived.
Overcame and tried to live again.
Not like I was before.
I was ever so much stronger.
Then I met you and again my life shifted.
You snuck pasty defenses with your kindness.
Trust and love shined in everything you did.
I learned to trust and love again.
The missing piece was found.
Now I'm better than ever.
For I feel whole once more.

Dreams

What do they mean?
What is trying to be conveyed?
Simple tricks of the mind.
Based on what you've seen and felt.
Or are they secrets that are untold?
Dark passages of sorrow and solitude.
Bright paths if joy and company.
So slip into your dreams for me.
Tell me what you see.
For I am longing for an answer.
What do they mean?

Without You

Life without you just isn't the same.
Nothing fits, the pieces aren't there.
My tears how they well up.
I weep until my eyes run dry.
Still I feel the pain.
Everyday it remains.
A hole in my heart that nothing can fill.
So I hold on tight, in the dead of night.
To my memories of days gone by.

Faithless

No matter how hard I try.
I just can't get anything right.
No matter how much I do.
It never seems to be enough.
What's the point of trying anymore?
Simply to learn the things I knew before.
Even if I try with all my might.
My best just isn't good enough.
Whenever I open my mouth.
It seems to make matters worse.
I might as well give up now.
I've got nothing left to sustain myself.
Why did I pin my hopes so high?
When I shouldn't have even tried.
I don't have kt in me to go that far.
I'm destined to fail, it's plain to see.
I just don't have any faith left in me.

True Worth

Happiness fills my heart, washing the darkness
away.
Love wraps its warmth around me, glowing like
embers of a fire.
Kindness falls on my soul, a gentle rain helping
it grow.
Trust builds a strong foundation, anchoring me
in stormy weather.
Faith in myself reaches up, a flower stretching
for the sun.
I have learned my true worth.
There's nothing out of reach.

Memories Linger

The day we met is so vividly clear.
That it might as well be yesterday.
Although we've said goodbye, everything
remains the same.
Each warm embrace, each stolen kiss, are
memories that linger still.
Years pass and feelings change.
Our love is not the same, but in a way remains.
Part of my heart is yours to keep.

My Nana, My Friend

It's times like this I miss my friend.
When it's late and I need that shoulder to cry on.
That one hug that makes the pain lessen.
Her voice telling me things will be okay.

I sit and listen, hoping to catch her singing.
Watching just in case she comes round the
corner.
Aching for her to call my name.
But only silence greets my ears.

So I'm left all by myself.
No one to tell my problems to.
My happiness kept to myself.
I sit and cry for all that's gone.

Time after time I've told myself.
She's gone and not coming back.
All I have is memories and her advice.
So I fall back on that instead.

It matters not how others see you, but how you
see yourself.
You can do anything you try.
And so her wisdom comes back to me.
Bringing with it a comforting warmth.

No longer am I all alone.
She's always in my heart.
Till the day I die, I'll always have my friend.
Through thick and thin she's been with me, my
Nana, my friend.

Escape

Trust shattered in an instance.
One moment seems like a year.
A lifetime of tears and overwhelming fear.
The darkness closes in and you forget the light.
Part of yourself lost forever.
Fantasy becomes an escape from reality.
That quickly became a nightmare.
Alone and scared you hide.
Closing off your heart.
To try and protect that tiny spark.

Starlight Dreamer

I am a starlight dreamer.
All my dreams come true at night.
I'm a lone star, shining bright.
I see the world through a veil of twilight.
Starlight flying through the night.
Starlight flying free.
Flying so low, all alone.
So high, no one to catch me if I fall from the
sky.
Once I became I had to learn.
You don't look back when you have the chance.
Can't have regrets after the price is paid.
Say goodbye to what I know.
Everything is gonna change.
Starlight flying through the night.
Starlight flying free.
Flying so low, all alone.
So high, no one to catch me if I fall from the
sky.
Don't look for help, no one's there.
From this day on I'm on my own.
During the day I hide away.
In the night I thrive and play.